MINI HACKS FOR

Pokémon

GO players

COMBAT

CATCH!
BATTLE!
COLLECT!

MINI HACKS FOR

PokéMon

GO players

COMBAT

SKILLS, TIPS, AND TECHNIQUES FOR CAPTURE AND BATTLE

JUSTIN RYAN

Sky Pony Press
New York

Sky Pony Press books may be purchased in bulk at special discounts for sales promotion, corporate gifts, fund-raising, or educational purposes. Special editions can also be created to specifications. For details, contact the Special Sales Department, Sky Pony Press, 307 West 36th Street, 11th Floor, New York, NY 10018 or info@skyhorsepublishing.com.

Sky Pony® is a registered trademark of Skyhorse Publishing, Inc.®, a Delaware corporation.

Visit our website at www.skyponypress.com.

10 9 8 7 6 5 4 3 2 1

Library of Congress Cataloging-in-Publication Data is available on file.

Cover design by Brian Peterson
Book design by Joshua Barnaby

Print ISBN: 978-1-5107-2156-2
Ebook ISBN: 978-1-5107-2160-9

Printed in the United States of America

TABLE OF CONTENTS

MINI HACKS FOR

PokéMon

GO players

COMBAT

INTRODUCTION

Pokémon GO boils down to two main functions: catching Pokémon and battling them. The world of catching is relatively simple: you have Poké Balls, you throw them at monsters, and based on their difficulty level and your own tools, sometimes you'll catch them and sometimes you won't. But catching in and of itself is a relatively simple thing to master in Pokémon GO. Battling, though, is a very different beast.

Electabuzz taking a beating
from Hypno.

Raichu getting psyched out
by Jynx.

Scattered throughout the endless maps of Pokémon GO are gyms where you are able to throw your Pokémon in the ring and duke it out with an AI version of someone else's masterful monster. You can train at gyms controlled by your own team, or you can attempt to conquer those being claimed by a rival squad. But to succeed at this battling challenge, your Pokémon will need to be top notch, the very best of the best, not just some random Charmander that hasn't been leveled up or a Pinsir whose Combat Power might not be as mighty as his claws suggest.

I'm talking about evolved, high CP Pokémon whom you know how to control and effectively use in battle. You'll need to know which opponents not to face and how to have a solid dodging defense to win.

If you think you've got what it takes to battle your way to the top of the Pokémon GO ladder and are not afraid to take a few punches along the way, like my Vaporeon here, then hop on in.

Vaporeon takes a hard punch from Electabuzz.

CHAPTER 1
GETTING STARTED

Battling first becomes available in Pokémon GO when you reach Level Five. At that point, you'll be given the option to join one of three teams: Team Valor, Team Mystic, or Team Instinct. Each team is represented by one of the three legendary birds from the original video game series: Moltres, Articuno, and Zapdos respectively. Team Valor values strength, Mystic is intrigued by evolution and tranquility, and Instinct is driven by intuition and egg hatching. No matter what team you choose, you'll be able to go up against the other two in battle, and you will be able to train against other Pokémon in gyms that your team currently owns.

Here you can see a gym which is currently controlled by my team, Team Valor.

There are no particular strengths or weaknesses to each team. Some people suspect that joining Team Instinct reveals rarer Pokémon when you're hatching eggs, or joining Team Valor will give you greater success in battle. But none of that's been proven, so choose whichever team you feel is best.

After choosing a team, you'll be officially able to go battle at any gym on the Pokémon GO map. But because you're only at Level Five, you probably won't fare as well against gyms that have more evolved and high-level Pokémon.

I joined Team Valor because I liked their red colors and I thought their values were the coolest.

Even if you do manage the impossible and topple a high-powered Vaporeon with just your meek Ponyta, your Pokémon will be too weak to defend that gym for a substantial amount of time against another player's monsters. You'll need to evolve and level up your Pokémon if you want to win.

This Growlithe is already pretty strong, but I'll need to evolve it to be a true contender.

CHAPTER 2
EVOLVING AND LEVELING UP

Two key ingredients are needed to evolve and level up your Pokémon: Candy and Stardust. Pokémon can have several evolutionary cycles, and they have specific candy that only they and other Pokémon in their evolutionary cycle can use. So a Charmeleon still needs Charmander Candy if it wants to evolve into a Charizard. This Candy can be obtained by capturing that specific type of Pokémon or another of its evolution type in the wild, or by transferring a Pokémon back to Professor Willow, who will give you one Candy for each.

Here you can see my Nidorino still needs four more Candy to evolve into a Nidoking, but it does have the necessary Stardust and Candy amount to power up.

Some Pokémon are easier to evolve than others. For Pidgey, you only need twelve Pidgey Candy to evolve it into a Pidgeotto, which isn't that hard considering Pidgey are common and can be found easily in grassy areas.

I have more than enough Candy to evolve this Pidgey, since Pidgey are easy to come by.

But for Ekans, you'll need fifty of its Candy to evolve it into an Arbok. And for some Pokémon with three evolutionary stages, like Charmander, you'll need twenty-five of its Candy to evolve it into a Charmeleon, and then one hundred Candy to evolve it into the ferocious Charizard.

Ekans needs twenty-four more Candy to evolve.

Charmeleon needs a whopping seventy-six more Candy to evolve.

Once you get enough Candy to evolve your Pokémon, make sure you select the highest CP version of that Pokémon in your possession. If you evolve a weak Rattata, it'll become a weak Raticate. But if you evolve a strong Growlithe, it'll lead to a strong Arcanine. Don't evolve more Pokémon than you need. While evolving is a valuable way to get experience points, it reduces the amount of Candy you have to actually level up your Pokémon.

I have more than enough Candy to evolve this Pidgey, but seeing how low its CP is, it probably isn't worth it.

To level up Pokémon and make them stronger, you'll need Stardust, which can be obtained by capturing monsters, hatching eggs, or defending gyms. Unlike Candy, Stardust is universal to all Pokémon. There are no different types of Stardust.

Now with enough Stardust and Candy in your stock, here's the difficult question: Which Pokémon do I power up, and how many Pokémon should I focus on powering up? Simply put, you want to power up the highest CP level Pokémon in your possession, but also Pokémon with the most potential, those who aren't just the strongest now but who'll be stronger later.

In terms of how many Pokémon you should focus on powering up, a good amount to start would be between six and eight and the max answer would be sixteen. Six is the amount of Pokémon you're allowed to battle with at enemy gyms, so having a strong team of high-powered Pokémon would be great.

If you reduce an enemy's gym prestige to zero, you have the option of selecting a Pokémon to place there to defend it in your team's name. However, you won't be able to use that Pokémon again in battle until you swap it, you remove it, or it is defeated.

I have about six Pokémon right now who could hold their own in a low-level gym, but if I want to beat some of the tougher opponents out there, I'll have to power my team up a lot more.

This is where things get tricky, as you'll want to select a Pokémon that is strong enough to hold its own against enemy combatants. But you'll also want to have enough in your inventory to claim gyms on your own. That's why sixteen is the max amount of Pokémon you should focus on powering up. You can only have one of your Pokémon stationed at ten gyms, max, at any time in the game. Add a solid six for when you go to battle enemy gyms or train at one of your team's gyms.

This Vaporeon is my favorite Pokémon to use in battle, but rarely do I ever station it at a gym because I wouldn't be able to use it and conquer more gyms as frequently.

CHAPTER 3
USING ELEMENTS TO YOUR FAVOR

Each Pokémon has an elemental type, and some have two. Most types are stronger or weaker to other certain types in battle. As you would guess, Fire Pokémon are generally weaker to Water Pokémon, but Water Pokémon don't really hold their own that well against Grass Pokémon. Elemental type doesn't really matter that much when your Vaporeon has five hundred more CP than a Jolteon, as your Pokémon will still have a much stronger attack despite Jolteon having the elemental upper hand. But when you're facing gyms that have Pokémon of different elemental types, you'll want to select a well-balanced team to match theirs.

A strong Vaporeon is a Flareon's worst nightmare.

Take for example this gym. It's currently being guarded by Flying types, a Pidgeot and a Dodrio. The Pidgeot is at a decent CP level, while the Dodrio is at a higher power level.

Since both are technically Flying types, it'd be wise for me to use a Pokémon like Raichu who excels at fighting Flying types, or my Vaporeon who has a very high CP.

Again, balancing CP and Pokémon type is a difficult process when battling. While it would make sense for you to send out your hordes of Water Pokémon to fight a gym that's primarily controlled by Fire Pokémon, if you have three to four Pokémon who are at a much higher CP than the gym's Pokémon, that will be more beneficial than just having better elemental types. Evaluate each battle situation differently and choose your Pokémon wisely.

Here I used strong Fire and Water types,
as well as Water and Grass types too.

To make my group more well-rounded, I could use
an Electric-type Pokémon like Jolteon or Electabuzz,
against which a Flying-type Scyther is weak or a Rock-
type Pokémon like Golem. But if Scyther's CP is lower
than all of my Pokémon regardless of type, I'll still
likely beat him in battle.

CHAPTER 4

BATTLING AT GYMS AND LEARNING TO DODGE

Winning battles at gyms controlled by rivals will reduce their prestige. Winning at gyms controlled by your own team will *raise* that gym's prestige. Reducing a rival team's prestige to zero makes that gym open for grabs. If someone reduces a gym's prestige to zero where your Pokémon is stationed, that Pokémon returns to your collection once it's defeated and the gym becomes up for grabs. Here I defeated all the Pokémon at this gym and now have the option of putting up one of my own.

You can tell a gym is up for grabs because it's colored silver, instead of one of the team colors.

Not all gyms are created equal though, as gyms level up, too. A gym with less than two thousand prestige is at Level One, making it easily conquerable, while a gym with fifty thousand prestige is at Level Ten, the highest it can reach, based off information from pkmngowiki.com. This is why you'll see some gyms frequently being handed over from team to team, but other gyms that are long-standing, with dedicated players who help raise prestige as other teams try to attack.

I'm pretty sure this same Arcanine has been at this gym for weeks now.

To conquer gyms, you'll ideally want to go after ones where the Pokémon's CP level is at the same level or close to those of your Pokémon. You're probably not going to defeat a Level-Ten gym with Pokémon who are below five hundred CP each, and you'll easily trounce a Level-One gym if you have six Pokémon with more than one thousand CP each.

At this gym, the Vaporeon is pretty strong, but I'm confident enough that my higher-powered Vaporeon will be able to put up a strong fight.

Battling really boils down to two things: knowing when to attack and knowing when to dodge. There might be situations when you'll only be able to squeeze in an attack every fifteen seconds or so because you'll be dodging a powerful Pokémon's blows. Other times you'll be so powerful you can literally just sit there and press attack over and over again while absorbing your enemy's weak attempts to hurt you. But in those situations where you are closely matched to an opponent, you'll need to dodge and attack at the perfect moments. On the following page, you can see I dodged the opposing Vaporeon's attack because of the message that appeared.

You can also see how my Pokémon moved to the left of Vaporeon.

Here I dodged a mighty Charizard's attack and that put me in good position to win the battle.

Many opposing Pokémon will attack two times in a row before taking a quick breather. Move consistently across the board as they attack, and you should be able to effectively dodge them. Special Attacks are harder to dodge. When a message appears like "Flareon used Heat Wave," that Special Attack looks a lot more menacing as it approaches you. You can also tell when a Pokémon is going to attack if there's a flash that appears in a circle on the edges of the screen. All of these can be dodged, if you effectively move at the right moment, when the flash appears. And of course, dodging isn't foolproof.

Even if you think you've dodged correctly, you still might absorb damage. The only way to master this is through practice.

Here you can see an example of the yellow flash, but it can happen so fast that you'll miss it.

Dodging, though, can only go so far if you're in a David vs. Goliath scenario. There's a timer that you also have to beat in the opposing gym. You can't just dodge and walk away a victor. Put yourself in a good dodging position and then it's time to attack! You can usually get in one or two strikes before your opponent starts attacking again, and depending on where you're located on the battle ring, you might have a chance to attack even more times. A Raticate who isn't looking directly at you has to turn around for it to attack. This means you have more opportunity to attack in that brief moment.

Based on the length of the dodging and attacking process, how badly your opposing Pokémon is damaging you, and how much time you have left, you can get a good gauge of whether you can win your battle. But if you're having difficulty, it might be time to take a break from battling, level up your Pokémon or train at your own gym, and get a better handle of battle mechanics.

Now here's the tricky part after you win: picking a Pokémon to defend the gym. Say you live in a neighborhood surrounded by lots of green space. Chances are there'll be a lot of Grass- and Rock-type Pokémon there, and chances are anyone who lives in the same neighborhood will also be catching and training them. So if you claim a gym in an area that's element-specific, it'd be smart to use a Pokémon that your opponents would be weaker to and one that would conquer the Pokémon that commonly appear in this area.

When I select a gym I just defeated, I can now see my Trainer with the monster I selected this time around, Pinsir. I don't mind not being able to use my Pinsir while it's at this gym, and I want to be able to use my Vaporeon to conquer other gyms.

The best possible type of Pokémon would probably be a rarer, Fire-type Pokémon like Charizard or Flareon, since the Grass Pokémon here would be weak to fire.

I went with Pinsir instead, and will probably see it back in my collection very quickly.

CHAPTER 5
SPECIALTY VS. REGULAR ATTACKS

Time is your greatest resource in battles. You can be a master dodger, but that won't mean much if you can't reduce your opposing Pokémon's HP to zero before the time runs out. This is where you should consider using a Special Attack.

Here you can see an enemy Vaporeon use one of its special attacks, Hydro Pump.

Each Pokémon has its own set of Special Attacks, and your Pokémon will have spawned with one of these three Special Attacks randomly. So for a Vaporeon, you can have one of its three Special Attacks, which are Water Pulse, Aqua Tail, and Hydro Pump. Depending on which Special Attack my Vaporeon has, I can use it when the blue bar underneath its name has reached a certain level. That blue bar charges based on how many regular attacks I'm able to pull off, regardless of how effective they are on the Pokémon I'm facing.

My blue bars are charged to take this Lickitung down.

Since you don't really have a choice on which Special Attack you can use, you need to decide if it's even worth using at all. Hydro Pump, the strongest of Vaporeon's Special Attacks, also takes a while to charge and can only be used once before it needs to recharged and you can use it again. Hydro Pump is very damaging to enemy Pokémon, while Water Pulse is not nearly as deadly. But I can charge Water Pump up more quickly.

Special Attacks are best used in certain scenarios. For Vaporeon, its Hydro Pump would be most effective against a Pokémon like Snorlax, who has a high defense and absorbs attacks with no problem. Vaporeon's Aqua Tail would be best served against a Fire type like

Arcanine or Flareon, since Aqua Tail recharges relatively quickly but is still damaging enough on its own. Some Special Attacks hurt a lot and some are also fun to watch.

One of my favorites is Arbok's Gunk Shot, where the snake actually throws a trash can at its opponent.

And let's not forget Nidoqueen's Sludge Wave, where a black pool of ooze bubbles up underneath the enemy Pokémon.

As you become more and more advanced in the game, Pokémon type will seem to matter less and less, as you face monsters at lower CP and defeat them with ease, even if your type is historically weak against them. But when you're facing a tough rival gym, consider choosing a mix of Pokémon not only with differing elemental types but also different levels of Special Attacks.

CHAPTER 6

DIFFICULT POKÉMON TO BEAT IN A GYM

Under the right circumstances, any Pokémon is difficult to beat in a gym. But here are difficult Pokémon you'll commonly encounter in game-play and how to top them.

Type: Flying, Rock

Watch out for: Aerodactyl is easily one of the most terrifying-looking Pokémon.

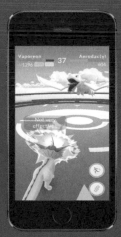

Iron Head will give you a headache but isn't necessarily a knockout.

Simply move around the creature and avoid its barrage of straight-on attacks.

Type: Poison

Watch out for: Arbok stings fast and hard, and its Special Attack Gunk Shot is hilarious, but it can be more harmful if you don't take it seriously.

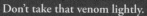

Don't take that venom lightly.   This snake knows how to slither.

Type: Fire

Watch out for: Arcanine may be one of the most common Pokémon you encounter at gyms, since his lesser-evolved form Growlithe is common in some areas, and spawns frequently for catching.

Arcanine also attacks quickly
and powerfully.

Arcanine's Bulldoze, while not as devastating as Rhydon's Earthquake, can still pack
a punch if the Pokémon's CP is high enough.

BLASTOISE

Type: Water

Watch out for: Arguably the coolest Pokémon, Blastoise squirts and stomps its way to battle victory. Its attacks can hurt twice as much, and Hydro Cannon is one of the deadliest among Water types.

Those water cannons are intimidating.

Not effective against Vaporeon, but deadly against others.

CHARIZARD

Type: Fire

Watch out for: That massive Charizard tail, which it uses to whip around and attack. One of its Special Attacks, Flamethrower, lives up to this dragon's fiery reputation.

Keep your eye on his tail, as it inflicts damage when you're not expecting it to.

Not effective against Vaporeon, deadly against others.

CLEFABLE

Type: Fairy

Watch out for: Adorable but clumsy, Clefable isn't the most graceful on the battle board and throws slow punches.

Clefable looks harmless but can easily pull mind tricks on you.

Psychic can be disorienting, so watch out.

Type: Flying, Normal

Watch out for: Drill Peck, which lasts a lot longer than other Special Attacks. This Pokémon takes a while in between its regular attacks, but when it is ready it strikes quickly, so be prepared.

This bird is a pecking nuisance.   Those darts are deadly.

DRAGONITE

Type: Flying, Dragon

Watch out for: Dragon Pulse, a massive beam that's utterly devastating. Dragonite is slow, but nothing really harms it that much, except for maybe another Dragonite.

Do your best at dodging, but you'll probably need to use one or two high CP Pokémon just to get past Dragonite.

When you see this, you've probably already lost.

Type: Electric

Watch out for: Electabuzz looks like it's constantly in a bad mood. It wallops punches with a fierce quickness, and its Special Attack Thunder isn't to be trifled with.

Electabuzz with the left hook!

My Vaporeon does not do well against thunder.

Type: Psychic, Grass

Watch out for: Exeggutor looks like a goofball but packs harsh regular and Special Attacks. Solar Beam is particularly dangerous, as it's easy to get caught off guard by the monster's goofiness before you're blindsided by deadly light.

Don't be tricked by Exeggutor's sad face.

He's about to throw some pain.

This special attack is quite painful.

Type: Fire

Watch out for: Heat Wave. If you're fighting with a Pokémon that's weak to Fire, like Grass, Ice, or Bug, it'd be better to swap out before Heat Wave overpowers you.

Flareon is cute but still will leave you with burn marks.

Not effective against my Vaporeon but effective against plenty of other types.

GOLDUCK

Type: Water

Watch out for: Hydro Pump. This affects not just where your Pokémon is standing at that given moment, but also the spaces next to it. Golduck's a slow-moving Pokémon in general, so you'll have more time to dodge and focus on attacks when necessary.

Golduck is one of the stronger Water monsters.

As is its Special Attack.

Type: Rock, Ground

Watch out for: Ancient Power. This Special Attack takes a while to charge up, so there's plenty of time to dodge it. Golem in general takes longer to prepare for each attack than most Pokémon.

Ancient Power sounds menacing, and it is.

Golem can be dodged, though.

Type: Water, Flying

Watch out for: Its Twister attack is menacing but avoidable. Don't be intimidated by this Pokémon's regular attacks either.

Gyarados can be easy to beat if you anticipate its attacks.

When you see this, you've probably already lost.

Type: Psychic

Watch out for: Psyshock. This Special Attack will surround your Pokémon with rocks and rays. All of Hypno's attacks in general are very hard to dodge.

Try not to get distracted and keep moving.

Hypno is summoning the rocks my way.

JOLTEON

Type: Electric

Watch out for: Out of all the Eevee evolutions, Jolteon seems to move most rapidly. Thunder, one of its Special Attacks, will catch you off guard as Jolteon will summon the blast near it and the blast will appear near your Pokémon. As soon as you see the word "Thunder" appear, begin dodging around the screen.

I'm doing pretty well, considering its CP is almost as high as my Pokémon's.

Don't ever send a Water-type Pokémon against a Jolteon if you can avoid it.

Type: Psychic, Ice

Watch out for: Jynx throws Double Slap with reckless abandon. The Special Attack Psyshock generates in front of Jynx, but later materializes in front of your player.

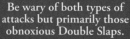

Be wary of both types of attacks but primarily those obnoxious Double Slaps.

Depending on CP and elemental weakness, Psyshock can be a bruiser.

Type: Rock, Water

Watch out for: Kabutops's regular attacks aren't anything to fret over, but its Ancient Power will send massive rocks towards your Pokémon.

Continue to dodge the rocks as they make their descent.

Its claws may be prehistoric, but they still cause a lot of pain.

Type: Water, Ice

Watch out for: Lapras is slow and sluggish, but has a massive defense and a killer Special Attack. Dragon Pulse is dangerous too.

Dodging Lapras is easy.

Well, maybe not for Special Attacks.

Take advantage of its poor speed, and attack fast.

LICKITUNG

Type: Normal

Watch out for: Hyper Beam, which is brutal. Lickitung's tongue lashes take a long time, so continue dodging.

Knock it down before he can get to its special attacks.

And maybe take a shower after that face licking.

Type: Fighting

Watch out for: Fire Punch. Machamp throws down the attacks as fast as any champion boxer, and moves quickly as well.

Machamp is big but don't be intimidated.

Dodging quickly and waiting for that right opportunity to attack is your best bet.

Attack fast, and quickly.

Type: Fire

Watch out for: Even though its entire body is covered in fire, you'll still need to watch out for Magmar 's regular attacks.

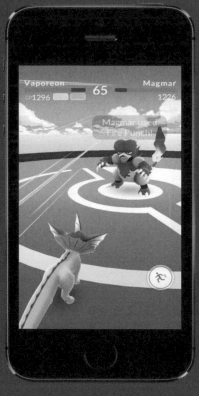

What you'll need to avoid is one of its Special Attacks, Fire Punch, which is even more damaging if your monster is weak to Fire.

Also avoid its regular attacks, in general.

Type: Ground, Poison

Watch out for: Brute force is the name of Nidoking's game. He hits you with attacks that'll make your head spin and then some.

Nidoking trying to establish his dominance.

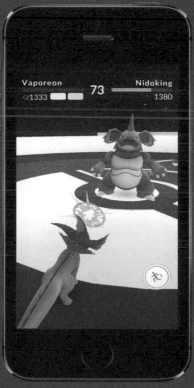

His Megahorn Special Attack is a straight on shot, so keep moving to the sides, attack when you can, and try to avoid those hurling punches.

Type: Ground, Poison

Watch out for: Nidoqueen packs the same toughness of Nidoking but with a particularly damaging Special Attack called Sludge Wave.

She's just as, if not more, hurtful than Nidoking.

Here black sludge will appear underneath your Pokémon, almost consuming them like a tar pit, so keep focused on what's happening under your Pokémon.

Type: Rock, Water

Watch out for: Omastar doesn't look intimidating, but it packs a punch that dates back to the Stone Age. Focus on dodging, especially its Hydro Pump.

Omastar is small but it stings.

Up there with the deadliest of the Water types.

Type: Flying, Normal

Watch out for: Pidgeot is quick, and a hard match if you're using a Ground Pokémon. Aerial Ace isn't too hurtful of an attack, depending on its CP, but shouldn't be taken lightly either.

You'll commonly see Pidgeots at gyms.

Having a fast Pokemon will benefit you greatly.

Type: Bug

Watch out for: Vice Grip. Pinsir's Special Attack comes in from both sides, fooling you into thinking that you've already missed your opportunity to dodge. You can still move quickly to avoid the attack.

Not the most
photogenic smile.

Move, don't stay still
when you see this.

POLIWRATH

Type: Fighting, Water

Watch out for: Poliwrath winds up before its hard-hitting punches and delivers them once or twice at a time.

Poliwrath's a bit slow, but its Hydro Pump can still cause a lot of damage.

Who knew a Water type could hit so hard?

Type: Fire

Watch out for: Rapidash's attacks are slow, but Heat Wave is disorienting. If the horse uses it, pay attention to light on the ground approaching you, as that'll be what inflicts the most damage.

Don't be fooled by its beauty.

Rapidash is a champion fighter.

Type: Normal

Watch out for: Don't worry about Raticate's regular attacks, even if it's at a higher CP (why anyone would bother leveling up a Raticate, I don't know.)

A nasty pest.

Hyper Beam, though, is not to be taken lightly, as the pest's Special Attack can knock you on your knees.

Do try to dodge it when possible.

Type: Ground, Rock

Watch out for: Earthquake. This attack overwhelms Pokémon in all directions and is immensely difficult to dodge.

Keep on Rhydon with fast attacks while dodging when necessary.

Watch out for Earthquake, one of the deadliest Ground attacks.

SANDSLASH

Type: Ground

Watch out for: Rock Tomb. Sandslash's attacks are all pretty easy to dodge, but like Psychic, Rock Tomb is a bit distracting, and getting caught up in the animation of the attack can end up leaving you hurt.

Sandslash digs in early.

And buries you with rocks.

SCYTHER

Type: Flying, Bug

Watch out for: X-Scissor. Scyther moves quickly with its regular attacks and X-Scissor is just the cherry on top. Using a strong Fire Pokémon will help bring him down.

Scyther flies and attacks quickly.

Using a strong Fire Pokémon will help bring Scyther down.

Type: Water

Watch out for: Don't mistake Seaking for the similar-looking, mild-mannered Magikarp. Seaking throws what look like wooden spikes at you, and does it quick.

Ouch, that hurts!

Arguably these attacks are more deadly than its Special Attack Wind, but be prepared for everything that comes your way.

Type: Psychic, Water

Watch out for: Slowbro is another goofy Pokémon that should still be taken seriously. It squirts water and jumps almost like a two-part attack.

Slowbro squirting some water.

And then a disorienting Special Attack.

The goofy Pokémon is pretty well-rounded.

SNORLAX

Type: Normal

Watch out for: Well, everything. Snorlax is massive and moves slowly, and many of your attacks will just feel like a soothing, harmless massage to it. Attack fast and do your best to avoid Body Slam, which is devastating because it happens quickly and will reduce your Pokémon's hit points to zero.

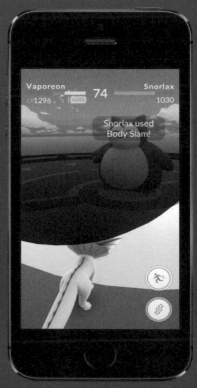

Tired of winning so many battles?   Body Slam can be overwhelming.

Type: Normal

Watch out for: Tauros tips back on its legs and fires a beam for its regular attack, which is strange, as you'd expect it to charge at you. One of its Special Attacks, Earthquake, causes damage across the board, so keep moving around and try to take Tauros out before it uses that move.

Tauros stampedes with its attacks.

And has a nasty Special Attack, Earthquake.

Type: Poison, Water

Watch out for: Tentacruel flings its tentacles at you while flying. Blizzard is a Special Attack that'll generate a few ice flakes, before your Pokémon is hit by a barrage of snow.

That's one nasty-looking fish.

Don't focus on the flakes and continue moving if and when that attack comes.

You don't want to be caught in the snow.

Type: Water

Watch out for: Hydro Pump. Just one of Vaporeon's Special Attacks but easily the deadliest, as this massive beam takes a big chunk out of your HP.

The aquatic attacks come fast with Vaporeon.

It takes a while for Hydro Pump to power up, so attack quickly.

Type: Bug, Poison

Watch out for: Psychic. This attack is equally hypnotizing and disorienting. Venomoth can generate a few purple rings near its head, and mirrorlike objects will appear near your Pokémon.

A blank stare doesn't mean you shouldn't take it seriously.

Don't get entranced; dodge when you have the opportunity.

But if you see the mirrors near your monster, you're going to suffer some damage.

Type: Poison, Grass

Watch out for: Vileplume is adorable, but has a poisonous bite. Try to attack it when its flower isn't showing. Solar Beam can be distracting too, and deadly.

Every rose has its thorn, except for Vileplume, who has one hundred.

It's hard to land attacks against it.

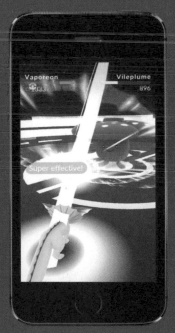

And one of its special attacks is blinding.

Type: Fairy, Normal

Watch out for: Cute but gets angry quick. Wigglytuff's Dazzling Gleam attack lives up to its name, making it easy to become distracted and get hit. Don't get entranced, and keep moving.

Cuteness aside, Wigglytuff is dangerous.

Don't be fooled by the smile; this Wigglytuff isn't your friend.

CHAPTER 7
BEST POKÉMON TO USE IN GYM BATTLES

A high-powered Electric Raichu would fare great against a tough Water Blastoise, but not necessarily against a supercharged Electabuzz. While CP should still be your guiding light in training and battling Pokémon, each monster also has a preset attack, defense, and stamina that remains at relative levels for all Pokémon of that type. So while a poisonous Venusaur might have incredible defense, it still will always be a slower Pokémon. Your Venusaur could be at a very high CP, but these traits remain consistent across the board.

Still, there has to be a certain group of Pokémon whose stats are top-notch enough that any apparent weakness quickly disappears in the shadow of their amazing strengths. Luckily the dedicated contributors at Silph Road, a massive, online network of Pokémon GO users, have spent countless hours learning the intricacies and nuances of the game. It's highly recommended you visit thesilphroad.com or reddit.com/r/thesilphroad (with a parent or adult's permission) to learn more about any specific Pokémon GO question or issue you may be having.

Based on information provided by The Silph Road and my own personal experience with the game, here are, arguably, the top Pokémon to use in battle. Some of these screenshots show the Pokémon in battle, while others are Pokémon I managed to get in my own possession.

ARBOK

Arbok has a pretty good defense and a decent attack, but what makes it a good Pokémon to consider is that Ekans, its lesser-evolved form, is generally one of the more common monsters you'll encounter in the game.

Because Ekans is so commonly found, you can evolve one quickly and power up an Arbok for battle.

Arcanine

You're bound to see countless Arcanines guarding gyms across your map, and for good reason. Their lesser-evolved Growlithes are easy to capture and power up with Candy. And they're great in battle.

Arcanine attack fast and powerfully with a pretty decent defense to boot.

BLASTOISE:

Arguably the strongest Water Pokémon, Blastoise has impressive attacks as well as one of the single best defense ratios in the game. This makes it great against pretty much any Pokémon, except Grass and other types that hold an elemental advantage.

A high CP Blastoise will probably crush anyone at the end of the day.

Each of these evolutions has a decent attack ability, with
Flareon holding the most strength potential and Jolteon
the quickest speed.

With Eevee being a common Pokémon to find in the wild, that means
you can power up each of these monsters faster than other high-ranking
monsters of their same types.

Golem

> Golem's a tough shell to crack with its impressive defense. Use it against a Pokémon that has a high attack percentage.

Golem is tough and well-built.

Flying, Water, and known for a high defense, Gyarados is a great fit to use against Ground- or Fire-based Pokémon, which really are some of the most common types you'll see at gyms.

Use this Pokémon against a stronger Fire type.

DRAGONITE

Don't let its friendly demeanor fool you; Dragonite is one of the most fearful Pokémon to go against. Its attacks and defense are among the highest of any Pokémon, and it is essentially weak to nothing except another Dragonite.

It's a little bit slow, but that won't matter when you're dominating opponents.

KABUTOPS

Top defense, great attacks, and the benefits of being both Rock- and Water-type give Kabutops an advantage over many different types of Pokémon.

A great Pokémon to use, in prehistoric times and now.

LAPRAS!

> Great defense and high CP capabilities make Lapras a valuable Pokémon against those with strong attacks.

Lapras are common at gyms for a reason.

MACHAMP!

Don't be fooled by the muscles; Machamp's best strength is its defense. Low stamina makes it a good choice against slower Pokémon with strong attacks but poor defenses.

Machamp strikes fear into the hearts of its fellow gym mates.

SNORLAX:

Capturing a Snorlax is almost like winning a mini-Pokémon lottery. Its defense is so incredible that all you have to do sometimes is absorb your opponents' attacks and just strike whenever you wish.

Snorlax moves quickly too, for being sso big, and holds very few elemental weaknesses.

Venusaur: High attack percentage, high defense, low stamina. But stay grounded with Venusaur and attack as quickly as you can.

Try to avoid Fire types, and you'll be on your way to victory.

CHAPTER 8
POKEMON TYPES' STRENGTHS AND WEAKNESSES

This chart shows if the elemental attacks of one Pokémon are stronger than or weaker than another type. To use this chart, find the type of Pokémon you want to use in battle or battle against in the attack column to the left. If you see a triangle pointing up, that means that Pokemon's elemental attacks are stronger against the defending Pokémon types listed across the top. If you see a triangle pointing down, that means they're weaker. If you see a blank space, that means there's a regular effect.

Top Row Key:

No = Normal	Fl = Flying
Fi = Fire	Ps = Psychic
Wa = Water	Bu = Bug
Gr = Grass	Ro = Rock
El = Electric	Gh = Ghost
Ice = Ice	Dr = Dragon
Fig = Fighting	Da = Dark
Po = Poison	St = Steel
Gd = Ground	Fa = Fairy

DEFENSE

ATTACK	No	Fi	Wa	Gr	El	Ice	Fig	Po	Gd
Normal									
Fire		▼	▼	▲		▲			
Water		▲	▼	▼					▲
Grass		▼	▲	▼				▼	▲
Electric			▲	▼	▼				✖
Ice		▼	▼	▲		▼			▲
Fighting	▲					▲		▼	
Poison				▲				▼	▼
Ground		▲		▼	▲			▲	
Flying				▲	▼		▲		
Psychic							▲	▲	
Bug		▼		▲			▼	▼	
Rock		▲				▲	▼		▼
Ghost	-								
Dragon									
Dark							▼		
Steel		▼	▼			▲			
Fairy		▼					▲	▼	

▲ = Super Effective

▼ = Not Very Effective

✖ = No Effect

DEFENSE

ATTACK

	Fl	Ps	Bu	Ro	Gh	Dr	Da	St	Fa
Normal				▼	✖				
Fire			▲	▼		▼		▲	
Water				▲		▼			
Grass	▼		▼	▲		▼		▼	
Electric	▲					▼			
Ice	▲					▲		▼	
Fighting	▼	▼	▼	▲	✖		▲	▲	▼
Poison				▼	▼			✖	▲
Ground	✖		▼	▲				▲	
Flying			▲	▼				▼	
Psychic		▼					✖	▼	
Bug	▼	▲			▼		▲	▼	▼
Rock	▲		▲					▼	
Ghost		▲			▲		▼	▼	
Dragon						▲		▼	✖
Dark		▲			▲	▼	▼	▼	▼
Steel			▲					▼	▲
Fairy						▲	▲	▼	

▲ = Super Effective

▼ = Not Very Effective

✖ = No Effect

So let's say we have a Water Pokémon like Squirtle that we want to use in battle.

If I look at this chart, I can see Squirtle's type, Water, on the left-hand side. I can then go across the row and see which of Squirtle's elemental attacks are stronger or weaker than the Pokémon on the top.

We see then that in the Water row, there are triangles pointing up for Fire, Ground, and Rock types, which means that Squirtle's elemental attacks cause more damage to these types. We also see that in that row, there are down arrows for Water, Grass, and Dragon types, which means that Squirtle's attacks wouldn't be as effective. This doesn't mean that Squirtle's attacks won't work against Water, Grass, and Dragon types, it just means they won't work as well.

Pokémon can also have more than one type. Jigglypuff is both a Normal and a Fairy type. Gloom, seen below, is both a Grass type and a Poison type. Pokémon with two types experience the relative strengths and weaknesses of both those types.

You can also use this chart to see if the Pokémon you're battling has elemental attacks that would be stronger or weaker against your Pokémon. Let's say you see a gym that's being controlled by an Electric Pokémon like Raichu and you want to battle it.

We can locate Raichu's type, Electric, on the left part of the chart, and then look at that row to see what its elemental attacks are stronger or weaker against. We can see triangles pointing up for Water and Flying types, and triangles pointing down for Grass, Electric, and Dragon types. This means we want to avoid using a Water or Flying type, since Raichu's attacks would be stronger than normal against them.

We could use a Grass, Electric, or Dragon type, since Raichu's elemental attacks didn't work as well against these Pokémon. But remember, if we used Electric, we would be in the same position as Raichu, since our Pokémon again wouldn't be as strong against an Electric type.

This is when we look at the top part of the chart and find the Electric type, and instead of looking left to right, we're going to look top to bottom and find the triangles pointing up. Those triangles will show us which Pokémon have elemental attacks that work well against Raichu.

In that column, we can see that there is only one triangle pointing up for Electric, and that is in the Ground row. This means if we have a strong Ground Pokémon, using it against Raichu would be to our advantage. We could also use a Grass or Dragon type, and although our attacks would work just fine, Raichu's wouldn't be as strong.

This chart is helpful when picking Pokémon for battle, but keep in mind that elemental attacks only go so far, and CP is still the main deal breaker in battle. So even if you see on the chart that your Fire-type Pokémon's attacks would have a bigger effect on a Grass-type Pokémon, that won't mean that much if that Grass type Pokémon is at a much higher CP. Same goes for if your Fire Pokémon was going against a Water Pokémon. Even if the Water Pokémon had the type advantage over you, you could still easily defeat it if your CP was higher than its. Also look to see the Special Attacks and damages Pokémon in each type have. Not all Water Pokémon are created equal, not all Fire Pokémon are created equal, etc. And some might fare better in particular battles than others, so look at how damaging their attacks are and work from there.

There are some interesting things to consider from this chart. A lot of Pokémon types are weaker against Steel, so if you find Magneton in your possession, it might be a good choice to defend a gym. Also Dragon Pokémon really only have a disadvantage against Fairy, Dragon, and Ice types, and aren't as strong against Steel types, but really are solid across the board for the other types.

Normal-type Pokémon, while not as exciting as other elemental types, hold virtually no elemental weaknesses except for fighting, since they don't really have any special element at all. That's why you see so many Snorlax defending gyms; they're great in battle and few Pokémon hold a significant advantage over them.

CHAPTER 9
CONFLICTS AND QUESTIONS

For the most part, battling in Pokémon GO can be a very fun experience. You train your Pokémon to the best of their abilities, you develop impeccable dodging and attacking skills to use in the heat of battle. If all goes well, you topple an enemy gym and claim it for your own team for as long as possible. But sometimes battling isn't all its cracked up to be. You might spend hours trying to take down another team's gym and not succeed, or put in the effort to power up your Pokémon even though there always seems to be another more experienced Trainer lurking around the corner. Here are some common conflicts and situations you may face when battling and what to do about them.

THERE AREN'T ENOUGH
GYMS NEAR ME

There are plenty of PokéStops around here–not to mention lots of Pokémon waiting to be captured— but there isn't a single gym in sight.

Although Pokémon GO is a game that's based on exploration, you're not always going to be able to travel far to find new gyms at which to battle. And that's when battling at the gyms immediately around you can become tiring. Try to map out gyms that are close to your area and that you can visit with a five- to ten-minute trip. This way you can expand the area in which you play the game on a regular basis. Any time your family is heading to the grocery store or out to do errands, join them on their journey and you can find new gyms you wouldn't be able to reach normally.

You can also try traveling to new areas and scouting out gyms there. If you're going to a family event that's thirty miles away, you can keep the game open on your phone and look along your route for any potential gyms you'll want to battle at on your way back, or even the next time that you visit.

THE OPPONENTS AT THE GYM ARE TOO TOUGH.

This Charizard's CP is more than five hundred points higher than my strongest Pokémon's, and the Trainer's level is much higher than mine. It's safe to say that I will probably not win this battle.

Lots of people have been playing Pokémon GO for a while, and some have become so good that it seems nearly impossible to defeat them at a gym. There are two things that you can do in this situation: continue powering up your Pokémon as much as you can and finally battle at the gym when you're totally ready, or just find a new gym to battle at. In Pokémon GO, you have a limited amount of resources, potions, and, most importantly, time to play the game.

With school, homework, chores, or other activities, you don't want to waste time being frustrated by losing gym battles when you could have fun fighting an easier opponent at another gym. Keep powering up your Pokémon as much as you can, but also know that there's no shame in walking away from a battle when you could be having much more fun playing somewhere else.

This doesn't mean that you shouldn't challenge yourself and fight opponents who might be tougher than you. Who knows? You just may end up winning. It's really just a question of how much time can you give to playing the game right then and there. If you win a battle and claim a gym for your team, are you ever going to be able to go back to that gym to battle again if your Pokémon get defeated? Explore and fight as often as possible, but make sure you're picking the good fights.

THE OPPONENTS ARE TOO EASY
OR NOT DIVERSE.

I was excited when I saw this Pokémon for the first time, but it's become more common as a gym staple.

Arcanine are easy to get and great to use in battle, so you're bound to see a bunch of these Pokémon defending gyms.

If you live in an area where there aren't that many gyms, or where fewer people are playing Pokémon GO, you might find that playing the game is too easy and that there aren't enough challenges for you. You might also find that there are a lot of gyms that have the same Pokémon defending them. If this happens, try to dedicate some time to finding new gyms outside of your area, even if they're just fifteen to twenty minutes away, so you can visit them regularly. You might also want to focus on just catching Pokémon while you wait for your opponents to catch up. One time, I went to all the gyms in my local area and claimed them all for Team Valor. It was fun, but I did it a few more times and then it wasn't quite as exciting since the opponents weren't really that difficult to beat. I only started to have a lot more fun when I tried to face different opponents in areas I wasn't used to.

I'M HAVING TROUBLE DODGING, OR THE GAME KEEPS FREEZING DURING BATTLES.

Sadly, you're probably going to find yourself in a situation at some point in which the game freezes or lags, and you'll end up losing your progress in battle. You can try to find a better cellular signal, or maybe a Wi-Fi network to connect to, but for the most part, you're just going to have to accept this setback and try again. The best Pokémon GO masters didn't become great after winning one battle; they had to deal with a lot of defeats and bad connections to get where they are now.

I've restarted my phone countless times since I started playing, and although it's an inconvenience, it's just something I need to do to keep playing the game. I'm not going to let that Pokémon I wanted, or the opponent I've been waiting to defeat, get away just because my connection isn't that good—and you shouldn't either.

I waited for five minutes here and the battle still wouldn't load. I had to restart my phone to try to battle again.

When it comes to dodging, sometimes it doesn't work, even if you're hitting left or right at the exact moment after the flash. There are two things you can do, if that happens: continue to time your dodges better or accept that you're not going to be able to dodge every attack. This is why you need a balance of strong Pokémon and good dodging skills when you go into battle. If you pin your hopes of winning on just trying to get that dodge exactly right with not-so-great Pokémon, you won't have a lot of success when you go up against tougher opponents. I've put a lot of time into getting very good at dodging but sometimes, even when I time it just right, dodging doesn't seem to work as it should. Balancing dodging with strong attacks is your best recipe for battle success.

CHAPTER 10
GET OUT THERE!

The only way you're going to get better at battling is by actually battling, so battle your heart out! Try to keep a steady amount of Potions and Revives available; you don't want to be caught in a position where you can't battle for a day or so because you can't revive any of your best Pokémon. Let CP guide you to glory. Maintain a well-balanced team of different types, attacks, defenses, and stamina.

And most importantly, learn how to dodge. Get good at it and time it perfectly. Beyond all the tiny details that go into making one Pokémon better than another in battle, dodging will ultimately be your strongest tool to avoiding attacks and staying alive. Conquer gyms far and wide, and let your monsters be true Pokémon GO champions!